To Collette,
in memory of
Getty Art

Maria Mazziotta [?]

THE GIRLS IN THE CHARTREUSE JACKETS

The Girls in the Chartreuse Jackets

WITH AN INTRODUCTION BY JAN BEATTY

&

POEMS AND PAINTINGS BY

Maria Mazziotti Gillan

CAT IN THE SUN BOOKS

First Edition

Cover set in Waters Titling Pro & Adobe Jensen Pro
Interior set in Adobe Jensen Pro

Cover Image: Maria Mazziotti Gillan, Women in Japanese Robes,
Mixed media on paper, 17" x 14 ½"

Book cover and interior design by Cassandra Smith

"We Used to Have Things We Believed in," San Diego Poetry Annual, 2011-2012.

Special thanks to Jan Beatty for her generous introduction, and to Mark Hillringhouse for photographing the paintings.

ISBN: 978-0-9911523-22

Cat in the Sun Books
5 Edgewood Road
Binghamton, NY 13903

Joe Weil, publisher
Emily Vogel, editor
Micah Towery, advisor

To all the strong, indomitable women in my life—

my mother, Angelina

my daughter, Jennifer

my granddaughter, Caroline

and to Diane di Prima,
who encouraged me to start painting again
and to let go.

TABLE OF CONTENTS

LIST OF IMAGES

Introduction

The Girls in the Chartreuse Jackets by Maria Mazziotti Gillan is a wondrous collection of poems and paintings that evokes the fire of being alive. There is *relationship* everywhere: the relationship between the seer and the world, between the woman speaker and her body—this is a woman-to-woman voice that embodies courage in these deep, moving poems.

Maria Mazziotti Gillan is one of the great poets and one of the great humans of all time. Anyone who has met her has come away changed by her fire, her electricity, her boundless courage and laughter. Reading this brave new work by Mazziotti Gillan, we feel the poems *breathe* in our hands and enter our bodies as she wows us with surprising imagery in the poem, "This Autumn": "…I throw off the gray cape through which I/have been moving, and I pull the flash and flame of the trees towards me…." We are transported to a relentless sense of being alive in the present moment, a moment filled with desire. And this transportation happens again and again.

I love the fire, the fierce womanhood, and sense of play that lives in these poems and lovely paintings: bright women's dresses, jewelry, and red, red lips color the paintings alive, and the floating dogs, cats, birds add whimsy and joy. This same wild joy runs through the poems of this book with evocative grace. Consider these lines from "This April, Nothing Goes to Waste": "Listen. I can almost imagine I hear the music/of a bird that sings in tune, and grief/can be forgotten for one moment/in the perfumed air." An elemental relationship forms between word and image as we move from poem to painting.

This would not be a Mazziotti Gillan book without the relentless sense of class, politics, and an authentic voice. The beautiful poems about Paterson show us the birth of an artist. In "My First Room in the 17th Street Apartment," we hear about "that tenement heated by a coal stove…My mother heated bricks in the stove and then put/them in the bed right before we ran to get into it." We meet relatives Zia Louisa and Zio Guillermo,

8

see the Royale Machine Shop where the beloved father was "both the janitor and night watchman." We see the great compassionate heart of this writer and the embrace of the difficult through precise, surprising detail.

The moving love poems to the mother, with her unforgettable voice, are stunning: "…Stop feeling sorry for/yourself. Just make up your mind to keep going." These poems are fiercely feminist, as Mazziotti Gillan writes strong women who are survivors, and writes them as a truthteller and risk-taker. We hear this first-hand in "Watching the River Rise": "…when we take a risk to reach out to/someone else, to tell the truth, we are almost dizzy with fear." This bravery, this feminism breathes through the women in her paintings, who appear as tough or pensive; as separate or together—we get a range of "real" women who are talking or dreaming or being—in the midst of moments of living. I love the sense of space in the paintings, giving these women room to move and also creating a feeling of possibility.

I admire the willingness to address great sorrow in poems of mortality and loss. In "What Does It Mean to Love You," Mazziotti Gillan addresses a husband of many years: "What does it mean to love you, even now, /that you are two years dead?/Oh ghost, oh shadow in the corner of my room." This is a writer who keeps the tough parts in, who looks eyes-open into the lonely night, and speaks about it with palpable emotion.

In "My Dreams Are Full of Women," the final poem in the book, we reach a pinnacle of tenderness and a delightful connection with the book's lovely paintings: "My dreams are full of women in bright dresses; they swirl around/a room filled with bright lights and birds…It's so sweet, isn't it? So sweet, and we are grateful." Yes, it is. It is so sweet, and we are so grateful to have Maria Mazziotti Gillan among us, with her gift of these amazing poems and paintings.

—Jan Beatty

This Autumn

This autumn, while the leaves on the trees catch fire, and the air
turns so clear and clean it could be water, I am shrouded in a grey
cloud, my spirit sinking with sorrow, loneliness solid as an apple.
How much more of my life will be lived in this solitude? How
much more grief will I have to learn to balance in my hand? I hear
my mother's voice in my head, hear her saying: "Just get up
and get moving," and I do—I throw off the gray cape through which I
have been moving, and I pull the flash and flame of the trees
towards me, lift the fallen leaves to my nose as though I could
erase all this sorrow in my life and fill it instead with such amazing
splashes of color—red, gold, yellow—like a gigantic impressionist
painting written across the sky.

Woman in Pink Dress with Flowers, mixed media on paper, 14" x 16 ½"

Woman in Blue Chair, mixed media on paper, 17" x 14 ½"

THE PATCHWORK QUILT

I've always loved patchwork quilts, the patterns
and colors interconnected and repeating, against
a snowy field. My mother is bright red, her body
electric with energy. When I think of her I imagine her
moving, her body rushing forward so fast
she is almost a blur. She is the red thread that races
across each pattern in the quilt of our lives, the pattern
she helped us create, so we'd always know
that each piece is dependent on the other.
My father is bright blue, set off against
my mother's red, his quick mind, his love of words
and numbers, his generous heart. My mother's
red holds the family together. My father's blue
is the ocean that reaches out to the world.
How they taught us to hold others with soft
hands; how they taught us
we could change the world. Each day, I wrap
the quilt around me, hug to me the way
they taught us to love everything
bent and broken and in need.

Women with Starry Eyes, mixed media on paper, 14 ½" x 17"

Look, the Fifties Weren't Anything Like That

The fifties were wide poodle skirts and crinolines, bobby socks
and saddle shoes, white bucks.

The fifties were dancing at the hop, ice cream sodas, and diners
with stools that swirled.

The fifties were Elvis Presley and "I Ain't Nothin' but a Hound
Dog," white nylon blouses worn with cotton full slips.

The fifties were boys in black leather jackets, standing
on the corner and making comments when we passed by.

The fifties were Eastside High School and teachers like Mr. Weiss
and Ms. Durbin, who made us believe we could do anything.

The fifties were hot dogs at Libby's near the Great Falls, parking
at Garrett Mountain Lookout, the lights of New York City visible

in the distance. The fifties were first kisses and first dances, "Love Me Tender"
and " My Funny Valentine" and all the other songs we loved.

The fifties were pouch bags and ballerina slippers, jalopies and old
Plymouths, fat and solid in colors like brown and maroon.

The fifties moved us through childhood into the teenage years,
shy, self-conscious, uncertain, the world both glittering

and dangerous, and I , my nose pressed to the glass, one foot
out the door, the other caught inside.

IN THE CITY OF DREAMS: PATERSON, NJ

I return to the block in Paterson, where we lived when I was
a child, that street with its two- or three-family houses, that street
with the raggedy apartment building on the corner where Irene
lived, Irene with her yellowed teeth, her torn clothes, wrinkled
and soiled, Irene whose family all looked like her, poorer
than the rest of us on the block because her parents drank
and the hallways of the building smelled of urine and where
my mother warned me not to go.

Across the street, Judy lived on the second floor over the bar
that her grandfather owned. Her grandmother and grandfather
lived on the third floor. Judy's apartment
had a big terrace, which was really the roof of the bar's
party room, and her parents had money. Between Irene's life
and Judy's, a huge chasm.

Past the old man's candy store, where we did not stop,
our house squatted. We lived on the first floor.
Zia Louisa and Zio Guillermo on the second.
Zio planted a huge garden so I almost believed
we lived in the country. Next to us
there were vacant lots filled with Black-eyed Susans
and daisies and wild grasses. Next to the lots
was Big Joey's house where we watched movies
in his backyard on his father's 16mm projector,
all of us sitting on folding chairs or on the grass,
all of us laughing at the cartoon characters prancing
and leaping across the screen. Across the street,
Little Joey lived, Little Joey who loved to write,
Little Joey who came to my reading last month
and I did not recognize him. He is almost as old as I am,
though I don't think of myself as old.

Sometimes, I think that little girl who played on 17th Street
is still playing hopscotch or hide-and-seek in the city
of dreams, all of us are still there, frozen in time,
the river stretching ahead of us wide and deep
as an ocean, summer days slow and easy, full
of games and the smell of flowers and Zio's tomato plants.
In the city of dreams no one dies. We are protected
and safe as though we lived in one of those snow globes,
where when you shook it, the snow fell over us
like small white flowers or stars.

Women Around the Kitchen Table, mixed media on paper, 14" x 16 ½"

MRS. PICARELLI

Mrs. Picarelli was lovely and fragile, a blonde, blue-eyed Italian
who fainted whenever she got upset, which was often.
Mr. Picarelli treated Mrs. Picarelli as though she was precious.
In our Italian neighborhood all the women,
except the very old, worked in the clothing factories
of Riverside, but Mrs. Picarelli stayed home, loved dressing up,
loved shopping, loved new hats and swirly dresses, loved her two
grown sons and her baby, Johnny, who was fifteen years younger
than Frank and Anthony, who were already married with children
of their own. Johnny wanted to be a priest.

But the young men who hung out on the corner near Burke's
candy store initiated Johnny into another club, one his mother
didn't know about, until after everyone in the neighborhood
knew, even the priests from the church, who told his parents they
should take Johnny to a psychiatrist to "cure" him, but that he
could never be a priest. Mrs. Picarelli cried
and fainted, cried and fainted, and Johnny tried to be "cured,"
to be married, to live a life everyone thought was "normal."
But there was always something caught in his eyes,
some yearning, some sorrow that he never spoke of
but that trailed behind him like a gauzy scarf.

Forties Woman, mixed media on paper, 17" x 14 ½"

MY MOTHER HAD NO COOKBOOKS

My mother didn't need cookbooks. By heart
she knew those recipes she learned from her mother
when she was a girl in San Mauro. I thought only
my mother could work her magic with food, but then
I go to San Mauro, and I find the exact food my mother
made, food as delicate and light as hers. Is it something
in the air or water? Is it something in their genes?
My mother brought San Mauro to America
and made it live in our house each time she rolled out
the thin dough for *le tagliatelle*, cut the dough into strips,
and hung it on a line until she was ready to slip it
into the boiling water in the huge pot on the old stove.
Or she'd form long ropes of dough, and cut it into small
pieces, and then with her thumb form *cavatelli*. I could
feel her mother and grandmother in that simple kitchen,
guiding my mother's hands and her heart.

At the holidays, weeks before Christmas, my mother bought
twenty pound slabs of chocolate, dried fruit, *pignoli*, *anisette*,
huge bags of flour, and she'd make *le pasticelle* and *struffoli*,
covered with honey and sprinkles. At Easter, she'd make
pizza chiana using dozens of eggs, ricotta, proscuito.

Ah, my mother was an artist, San Mauro in each movement
of hands, San Mauro in homemade bread, San Mauro in polenta
steaming in its bowl, San Mauro in stuffed artichokes, San Mauro
in *ragù* made with tomatoes she canned each summer, *ragù*
with crab, *ragù* with calamari, *pasta fagioli*, spinach and potatoes,
I never saw San Mauro until I was well into my sixties. My mother
never saw her mother again once she left San Mauro; she never
went back until after my brother graduated from medical school,
but she brought it into our house in the San Mauro food she

cooked, the fragrance and flavor of it, so when I go to San Mauro,
meet my first cousins for the first time, I'm sure I know them,
and I can hear in them that San Mauro litany,
that love of food, of feeding others, of presenting food
like a colorful gift to all who arrive to sit at the table,
so they will know they are welcome.

Window with Big Bird, mixed media on paper, 14" x 16 ½"

WHY I FAILED CHEMISTRY

I hated Chemistry because it made me feel stupid.
I couldn't learn the periodic table. Every time, I started
to memorize it, I'd go off into daydreams and realize
a half hour had passed and I'd learned nothing.
I was a senior. I was terrified I'd fail. The other day,

I met another poet and she told me, "I hated Chemistry.
I couldn't learn the periodic table." We both laughed,
though we weren't laughing then, those incomprehensible
letters and numbers impossible for us to memorize.

My brother has his Ph.D. in physical chemistry. His son
has a Ph.D. from Harvard in theoretical chemistry
and is a professor at the University of Chicago.
Their dissertations are page after page of formulas
devoid of even one word I understand. Luckily for me,
I didn't have to study chemistry ever again,
although I'm still ashamed of being defeated
by that dreaded periodic table that was printed
on a white shade that rolled down over the blackboard,
and that blurred and grew foggy
the moment I looked at it.

Woman in Orange Dress, mixed media on paper, 14" x 16 ½"

THE PICTURE OF THE THREE OF US

We had a Brownie camera when I was about eleven,
but my mother didn't believe in wasting money,
so I have very few pictures of myself as I was growing
up and almost none of my mother and father.
So the few pictures that remain are clear to me,
as though I could actually hold them in my hand,
although I am three hours away from home.

In one, I am sitting on the back steps of the tenement
on Fifth Ave in Paterson where I was born.
I must be about a year-and-a-half old. I am wearing
overalls and my hair is a curly cap on my head.
It looks blonde, but I know that can't be right,
and is just a trick of the sunlight and a cheap camera.

In another picture, I am about eleven. My hair is kinky
and sticks out from my head like a wiry tent. I am
uncomfortable in my own skin and it shows. In another,
my mother is sitting on the steps of the back stoop
at the 17th Street house. She is in her thirties. My brother
is sitting next to her. He is about eight and has on his baseball
uniform. She has her arm around him, her legs crossed.
She looks vibrant and sexy and foreign
with her dark skin and eyes.

Some door-to-door salesman convinced my mother
to part with money to have studio photographs taken,
and later to have the three photographs joined together
and tinted and framed. There we are, my beautiful,
older sister, her creamy complexion, her rosy cheeks,
her large dark eyes. My brother is wide-eyed and serious,
his hair in a bowl cut, his forehead high.

Between them, my hair springs into curls on my head,
my eyes wide opened and sparkling. I am not pretty, but I look
electric, like I can't wait to move, to get on with it, my energy
palpable even in a photograph.

Women in Japanese Robes, mixed media on paper, 17" x 14 ½"

Girls Playing Dress-up, mixed media on paper, 20 ½" x 16 ½"

CHEAP SHOES

My mother always made me wear Buster Brown shoes,
saddle shoes, white with a brown or black band in the middle.
The laces were white and black. My mother thought they were
good for my feet, and though I wanted ballerina slippers, those
soft-sided shoes with their thin soles, my mother said, "No, they
have no support." But all the girls in seventh grade had them
and they were pretty and cool-looking in a way that Buster Brown
shoes were not. That spring, when I turned twelve, my mother
bought me a pair of Mary Jane patent leather shoes
for dress up. They were not leather like the Buster Brown,
but a cheap version of Mary Jane's that would last for one season
of Sunday masses. One day, the Girl Scouts took us on a trip
to New York City, and I wore my patent leather shoes. The bus
took us to Times Square and dropped us off, and we walked
around mid-town, four or five girls with one adult. We went
to Radio City Music Hall, and then walked up 5th Avenue
to look at the Christmas displays. After a few blocks of walking,
the cheap Mary Jane's dug into my heel and made a large blister
that hurt every time I took a step, and bled onto my white socks.
I pretended nothing was wrong, kept trying to encourage
myself to keep going—one more block, two more,
and longed for the well-fitting, soft leather of my Buster Browns,
ugly, safe, shoes meant for walking and not these insubstantial
shoes like so much that is all surface and shine
but never lasts.

IN THE SEVENTH GRADE

In seventh grade, I wanted desperately to buy a chartreuse
satin jacket that all the cool girls in the class had. I thought
those jackets were beautiful, so shiny and soft,
and in that wild color that was so popular that year.

My mother said, "No, you don't need that junk,"
and looking back I see how cheap and sleazy
those jackets were, how that color would have made
my olive-toned skin look jaundiced, but then I fell asleep
dreaming my mother bought me that jacket,
and I'd slide my arms into the sleeves, and miraculously,

I would become one of the cool girls, the girls who stood around
on Paterson street corners with boys in black leather jackets,
the girls who would be the first to be kissed, the first to go out
on a date, the first to wear a boy's ring on a chain
around their neck, and not someone like me,
shy, inarticulate, introverted and unable to find even
one word to say to the boys in the class who treated me
as though I were breakable,

something in my big eyes and obvious innocence
that made them want to protect me. In seventh grade,
I wanted to be sexy and to have that quality some girls had
that drew boys to them, like bees to honey, the musk
my friend still has, where men flirt
with her and where her whole body changes
when she talks to them. Though seventh grade is an old
memory in black and white, some part of that child remains,

wanting a pill that could transform me, while the other part
of me, the one that races through my life like the Road Runner,
the one who has long since left that 17th Street tenement
behind, knows I would not trade the woman I have become
for all the shiny, chartreuse jackets in the world.

What I Lost, What I Can Never Have Again

I'd go with Jimmy, my first boyfriend, to Johnny and Hanges
in Paterson to get hot dogs and French fries. Sometimes, we'd go
on double dates with Lois and Bill. They always had the back seat.
They seemed to eat very quickly, and then I'd hear noises and
huffing breath. I didn't dare turn around.

Jimmy and I would neck in the front seat, the steering wheel
always slightly in the way between us. He'd place his lips
on my lips. I felt nothing. I didn't understand that a kiss
was supposed to be more alive than that, more electric,
and even when Jimmy tried to tell me he was gay, I didn't
understand. He wanted me to go with him to a gay club.
I said no.

His father was mean and sarcastic. He tried so hard
to be the man his father wanted him to be.
When I went to dinner at his house, his father was cold
and cruel. Jimmy held my hand, touched my shoulder.
Pretend. Pretend.
We broke up.

I started dating someone else, and discovered kisses
that lit up my body like an electric heater. Jimmy moved
to San Francisco. He wrote to me for a while, then no more.
I would think of him, sometimes, how terrible for him to have
to try to please his father, a man he could never please,
no matter what he did. If I could, I would tell him how sorry
I still am that it took me so long to understand, my sweet
sixteen self who had never been kissed until Jimmy,
who must have felt like he was kissing a creature
as unappealing to him as a frog or a stone.

Women and Flowers, mixed media on paper, 14" x 16 ½"

My Mother's Tough Love

My mother used to wash our sheets in cold
water in the wringer washer and hang them out
in the sun to dry. In bed at night, I'd breathe the pure
aroma of sun and fresh air.

My mother used to come to my house when I was teaching
to clean, and when I came home I knew she'd been there,
the kitchen polished and shining, the house smelling
as fresh as the sheets of my childhood. She'd call me and say,
"What did I do wrong? I spent six hours cleaning your kitchen."
She disapproved of my house, dust balls and lost shoes and books
and mounds of paper. My mother used to take our clothes home
to wash and she'd call and say, "What are you people doing?
I had to wash the clothes three times to get them clean."

My mother used to open her back door to me, scowling
and complaining, "Why didn't I stop working? Why didn't I do
things the way she did them? Why wasn't I neat and clean?"
But when I'd sit at her round kitchen table, it was my mother
who held my hand, my mother who served the food I loved,
my mother who offered comfort and espresso, my mother
who held me saying, "Cry, cry, it will be good for you."

Woman in Emerald Dress, mixed media on paper, 16 ½" x 14"

THE FIRST TIME I GOT DRUNK

At a college party, I met a boy from another college,
handsome in a blond American way. He flirted with me
and because he was so self-confident, so certain
he could choose any girl he wanted, he talked me
into having a whiskey sour. I remember a gleaming bar
with a mirror behind it and row after row of liquor bottles,
and the whiskey, covered by the taste of orange juice.
It was crowded in the room and Frank Sinatra
was on the jukebox, "My Funny Valentine"
and "Saturday Night Is the Loneliest Night of the Week",
and the young man hauled me onto the dance floor,
and talked me into another whiskey sour and then another
until the room spun and my eyes drifted unfocused
over this crowded room and he bent to kiss me. I kissed him
back and later I seem to have lost a block of time somewhere,
I was in a car and my friends drove me home. I rolled the car
window down and let the cold air wash my face,
as I tried to think about how sick I felt, and even when
I get home to our small house with its one bathroom
right off the kitchen, and I was sick and sick again
while my mother hovered over me, asking what happened
and I kept repeating never again, never again, as I leaned over
the bowl. I have forgotten that boy's name
and what he looked like, but I do remember,
even though it was more than fifty years ago,
the burn of bile in my mouth.

Japanese Women, mixed media on paper, 14 ½" x 17"

Our neighborhood in August...

meant chasing fireflies through vacant lots that were knee deep
in daisies and Black-eyed Susans and wild grasses.
In the late 40s, 17th Street in Paterson didn't have that city feel
to it with the Riverside oval on one end and two
and three houses lining the street, the front garden small
with statues of the Blessed Virgin and rose bushes,
or the back and side yards transformed into the immigrant's
garden. In our neighborhood in August, we played stickball
in the street or hopscotch or jump rope on the sidewalks,
and as dusk slipped its veil over the neighborhood, the kids, Judy,
Little Joey, Big Joey, my brother, sister and I retreated
to our back stoop. Zio Guillermo's garden filled the entire back
yard guarded over by the wind pointers and bird houses he built,
the tassels of corn whispering as they blew
in the wind. Our neighborhood in August was free and open,
the smooth wood of the porch under our legs, the swell
of ripe tomatoes and cucumbers and lettuce, the sky above us, a
huge black bowl crammed with stars, chunky as blocks of ice, how
they glittered and sparkled above us so close we almost believed
we could pluck one from the sky and slip it into a pocket, like a
lucky charm, and carry it with us forever.

THE ROYALE MACHINE SHOP

My father worked at the Royale Machine Shop for years. He was both the janitor and night watchman. Last week, filmmakers took me to the machine shop because I mentioned it in a poem, and they shot footage of me reading my poem with the factory in the background. The day after we go there, they send me photos taken that day with Royale Machine Shop on a bronze plaque in the background. The photographer talks the owners into letting him photograph the inside. When I look at the pictures for the first time, I think of my father cleaning that huge space and dragging his crippled leg through his nightly rounds. Was he afraid? He never said. A few days ago, they demolished the factory. The owners did not want to pay the taxes for a building that was empty. The Historic Preservation Commission tried to stay the demolition, but the city refused to waive their taxes, so now, a factory built in 1888 is gone. In its place, only dirt and rubble.

MY FIRST ROOM IN THE 17TH STREET APARTMENT

My first room, or the first one that I remember, is the one
on 17th Street in Paterson, that tenement heated by a coal stove,
huge and black, a stove with four flat burners right over the fire,
burners that my mother lifted off the stove with a tool
with a curved handle. The stove was in the kitchen. It heated
the apartment, though it really only heated the kitchen,
and that part closest to the stove was warmest of all. In winter,
the door to the tiny living room was kept closed and we all sat
together at the kitchen table to talk or read or do our homework
or play Monopoly or dominoes. My first room, the one I shared
with my older sister, was off the kitchen. It only had enough
room in it for an iron bed, not the fancy iron beds they sell
in antique stores, but plain and brown and utilitarian
like the kind of bed in a charity hospital. It was three-quarter
the size of a full-size bed, which would not have fit in the room.
My mother covered the bed with a plain cotton coverlet,
an imitation chenille with nubs that had been washed flat.
Next to the bed was a small dresser, also brown. On the wall,
a crucifix. My room had one window, warped, so wind blew in
and ice crystals formed patterns on the glass, patterns that looked
like lace. My mother heated bricks in the stove and then put
them in the bed right before we ran to get into it. That was
the room where I rested when I had the measles and had to stay
for days in the dark, because my parents were afraid the measles
would blind me. That room where I read my first books, the room
where my sister, so much more outgoing than I, would tell me
about her friends and about playing baseball with the boys
on 25th Street with my cousin and his friends, while my mother
asked everyone if they knew where my sister went after school.
Our upstairs neighbor asked where I was, because my mother was
so frantically searching for Laura. "Oh, Maria," she said,
"she's in her room reading."

I Did Not Understand

I did not understand why my mother called me every day.
"How are you? How are the children?" and then she'd hang up
without saying goodbye. When I asked her why,
she'd say, "I just wanted to find out if you were okay."
My busy mother, no time to waste with hello or goodbye,
though as soon as I needed her she'd appear at my door
with a pot of soup or homemade bread, ready to help me
in and out of bed if I was sick or nurse me back to health.
Now, that I have grown children of my own, at last
I understand why I call them just needing to know they
aren't hurt or sad, happy to hear my son's voice
on the phone, even though he's so far away I'll never
get him back, my daughter's voice, even when I can hear
that she has been crying. I love to hear her voice
when she is excited about some new project
or when it rises with hope. I know my mother felt
the same things about me, the way we all
want a magic potion that will make our children happy,
want to soothe all their scrapes and bruises,
as though our hands had in them the milk of the aloe
plant that could heal all wounds.

Two Birds and a Bouquet, mixed media on paper, 14 ½" x 17"

How the Dead Return

Ma, sometimes I feel that you are with me
each day, though you've been dead
eighteen years already, my life
slipping away from me like water
in my hands. Why is it that you
are the one I think of always
when I am afraid or tired,

you are the one whose voice prods
me forward when all I want is to crawl
into my bed to hide. Yours is the voice
that says stop feeling sorry for yourself,
you think you have it hard?

When I look at Dennis sliding down
in his electric wheelchair, his head bent
like the broken stalk of a tiger lily
or a gladiola, eyes terrified and pleading.
When I find I can't stand one more health aide
or handyman in the house,

when I am tired of so many people who need me,
no one for me to turn to for comfort
except you, Ma, you, and you come to me
as though you were still alive. Sometimes,
I can smell you, vanilla and flour and sugar,
you with your bread dough rising in its bowl,
you bringing me dishes of pasta or cups of espresso,

I swear I can close my eyes and conjure you up,
and for a moment, it's your arms I feel around me,
your hands in my hair.

WHY IS IT WHEN I THINK OF US, I REMEMBER

First, that picture of our wedding day,
we are posed looking out the curved window
of the limo my father rented for us,
our faces close together,
me, wide-eyed and happy in my white veil,
you, handsome in your black tux.

At my boyfriend's house, that night
when I saw you for the first time,
that night when everyone else faded
to shadow in that brightly lit room,
only you clear to me in your blond crew cut,
your blue-gray eyes, your broad shoulders
bent over your guitar, your strong voice singing,
"Black Is the Color of My True Love's Hair."

How fortunate to have the certainty that you
were the man I'd love all my life, though I felt
so guilty about falling for you so completely,
in an instant, guilty that I hurt my boyfriend
who had invited me home to have dinner
at his house and you, his best friend
since three, to his house to meet me.

How fortunate, that girl in her wedding clothes,
how fortunate that the feeling that exploded
between us like lightning is still there,
even forty years later, so fortunate
that the handsome young man
in the limousine window is the one
I still see when I look at you.

We Used to Have Things We Believed In

We used to have things we believed in, names
for all the things that were larger than we were,
more beautiful. When did I stop believing
the world could be saved, stop thinking
that it would never explode like the fire
that rises up in Cairo after a grenade hits a car?

We used to have things we believed in, names
for all the things larger than we were, more beautiful.
In my secret pocket, I still carry all the things
I have loved—the dark hump of the Catskills
that circle Route 17 West as I drive
toward Binghamton, the way my spirit lifts
at such raw, unspoiled beauty, each season
a different color, each season a new picture
caught in my mind, precious and eternal,

or the moment driving through the French countryside
when I saw field after field of sunflowers, their heads
proudly lifted toward the sun, or in the museum
in St. Petersburg, Russia, where I came upon room
after room of paintings by Matisse and Van Gogh.
How glorious and unforgettable.

We used to have things we believed in, names
for all the things larger than we were, more beautiful.
Though I can look around me, see so much ugliness
and war, famine and drought, evil and selfishness, part
of me still believes those exquisite moments
can save us, the memory of a child's face lifted
toward us, the sun glowing on the brick walls
of old mills, the moment on a mountain outside

of Taos where we turn a corner after having risen up
out of the red desert and find ourselves in a grove
of birch trees as though we had leaped
from New Mexico to New England.

I know that I'm naïve to believe that nature
and art and love can save us, but I cannot let go
of the notion that caring enough
about the world will help us to stop
all that destroys the beauty
that lights the world from within.

I SHOULD WRITE A POEM...

about all those people dying in Darfur,
but instead I listen to Joe saying he lost
his cell phone again and he worries
whether he dropped it in his toilet,
and I think how can someone who writes
poems so powerful they leave me breathless,
the words pitch perfect, be unable to hold
onto phones and belts and wallets and books
and receipts, all these things that should be
easy to keep, instead disappear into a void
that opens around him.

Women and Doves, mixed media on paper, 14" x 16 ½"

MY GRANDDAUGHTER AT NINETEEN

My granddaughter is nineteen and in her freshman year
at a university she hates. She tells me she wants
to transfer, has made no friends. She and her roommate
do not talk to one another. "I spend a lot of time
at the library," my granddaughter says. "I can't stand
being in the room with her." My granddaughter loves vintage
clothes; she's five foot eight and slender with very long legs.
She copies the hairdos and clothes of movie stars
from the thirties and forties. Underneath her sophisticated
exterior, her carefully styled auburn hair, she's shy
and bookish, quiet and afraid. My daughter says
that her exterior self doesn't match her interior one.
She looks cool and isn't. She works too hard and cares too
much about following the rules and getting high grades.
"Men always find that out about me eventually,"
my daughter tells me. "They think I'm cool and fun
and after awhile, they find out I'm serious and shy and quiet
and not fun at all."

Crazy Bird, mixed media on paper, 14" x 16 ½"

THIS APRIL, NOTHING GOES TO WASTE

This April, nothing goes to waste.
The air soft and perfumed caresses
my face and the meadows go wild
with flowers. The pear tree magically
blossoms pink, the forsythia waves
its small yellow hands at the highway's edge,

the world alive with daffodils and tulips.
What can we do but bow our heads
before such gifts? We know winter still
waits for us with its avalanche of ice and wind

but what does it matter today
when we cannot help but smile at the grace
of sun sparkling off water in the fountain,
the lily's trumpets lifted and blaring.

Listen. I can almost imagine I hear the music
of a bird that sings in tune, and grief
can be forgotten for one moment
in the perfumed air.

Watching the River Rise

I pull into the parking lot at the Paterson Great Falls National Historic Park, and listen to falls roaring like an enraged monster, though they gleam silver and beautiful, setting off a cloud of spray, the rain falls like polished pewter, pounds the blacktop, the river, muscular and fast, carries with it broken tree branches that lift out of the hurling water like arms. How alive the Passaic River is on this rainy spring day, even the statue of Alexander Hamilton watches the falls, though Hamilton appears unmoved, standing on his pedestal where he has stood for years. I remember the scene from The Sopranos, where they threw a man over the ledge into the water, and I look at the falls and the delicate bridge that spans the water. I have never climbed on it, I am afraid of heights and the bridge seems too slender to hold my weight, but I love this spot, love to watch sunlight shimmer off the falls. How much of our lives are like that, when we take a risk to reach out to someone else, to tell the truth, we are almost dizzy with fear, balanced on the thin bridge of our own vulnerability, willing to take a chance, to step on the span that could lift us to the other side or let us fall into the rapids below.

Woman in Blue Hat and Butterflies, mixed media on paper, 17" x 14 ½"

ON THE TRAIN FROM SWANSEA

The train picks up speed as it leaves Swansea station, passing
the chimney pots, lined up like soldiers on the attached houses.
Even now, months later, I celebrate them
for their orderly beauty, so neatly arranged, row after row
of Welsh houses, the sun brilliant in the sky, startling blue
with its puffy clouds. Beyond the ochre fields, dark green grass,
the soft mound of hills, the sunflowers. Wales with its lovely,
polite, welcoming people, Wales with its poets and music,
Wales with its sea birds that swirl and dip
above the chimney pots and houses.

WAITING FOR MY PRESCRIPTION AT TARGET

I am waiting for my prescription to be filled at Target
when the clerk suggests I walk around the store and shop.
"Twenty-five minutes," she says. "Maybe a little faster."
I, who hate to wait anytime, push the cart around Target, though
there's nothing I want. It's only 9 a.m., and I'm impatient,
annoyed already, though I know I need to be grateful
that my brother is a doctor so I could call him last night
and ask for a prescription for Librax, which I've been taking
for forty years to calm my nervous stomach. The original doctor
who prescribed it called it a "stomach tranquilizer" and it never
occurred to me that it was a euphemism for tranquilizer, and so
when the pharmacy in New Jersey did not deliver it, I just left
without it and all week I've been getting more and more tense,
and yesterday in class I cried three times, couldn't control
my voice or the tears, and when I tell my brother he says,
"Of course, you're in withdrawal from the pills." He calls in
a prescription. That's why I'm here at 9 a.m., worried that I won't
get to my class on time, and the store, even so early on a Sunday
morning, has people in it, as though Target has become the new
church—Oh praise to consumer goods, praise to miles of clothes
and kitchen equipment, praise to rows of over-the-counter
medications, praise to lamps and sneakers, praise to pillows
in bright colors and pocketbooks and chenille bedspreads.
There's a space inside us bigger than the Grand Canyon,
and no matter how much we buy, nothing fills it up.
The people wandering the aisles seem lost, their eyes dazed.
I remember when my children were babies, we lived in married
student housing at Rutgers, and I didn't know anyone that first
year, the days seemed endless, the apartment walls leaned
toward me, and I'd pack the children into the car and take them
to Bradlee's, Jennifer in the baby carrier I'd lift into the front
compartment of the shopping cart, and John in the cart itself,

sitting cross legged, holding whatever I bought, though since
Dennis's fellowship only paid twenty-five hundred a year, I never
bought much. I'd wander up and down the aisles on Bradlee's
black and white linoleum and try to pretend I was happy,
not lonely and afraid. I loved the children but felt my life
snapping closed around me as though I'd never escape.
Sometimes, I'd look up, meet another woman's eyes
and recognize that she, too, is walking these aisles to keep
from knowing where her life is going. Dennis was happy and busy
with classes and papers and teaching. I wrote college review books
during the children's naps and after they went to bed. I was so
bored I thought I'd die and this store today reminds me of that
time in my life. I can still see the slender girl I was, tears running
down her face as she walks Bradlee's aisles with her children,
and tells herself to be grateful for everything she has,
remembering what her mother said, "Stop feeling sorry
for yourself. Just make up your mind to keep going."

Woman at a Garden Party, mixed media on paper, 20 ½" x 16 ½"

Today, when I read the poems...

I start to cry. When a poem works,
I tell my students, it makes you cry, and certainly
this morning, one less layer of skin to protect me
from the poems, their blade of truth pressed
to my chest, everything about my own life
comes rushing back at me like that huge stream
that courses through the Catskills in spring, all
the times I lied to myself to keep from knowing
what I didn't want to know. Only poems can bridge
the rushing water of memory, give us a way to see
the terrible moments that stick up out of the past
like jagged rocks.

What Does It Mean to Love You

What does it mean to love you, even now,
that you are two years dead?
Oh ghost, oh shadow in the corner of my room.
I still meet you at the head of the stairs, see that you
are reaching out from beyond to let me know
I am not alone in our empty house. I still sleep
on my side of the bed, as though you
are still next to me.

What does it mean to love you, you who were with me
forty-seven years before you died, leaving me behind
in the house that rattles and shakes around me, emptiness
floating from the corners of every room, while I hide
behind the French doors to the family room, that room

where your shrine sits in its place of honor, surrounded
by pictures of us together when we were young, that room
where I read and write poems and watch BBC programs,
and forget that I am alone so I turn to laugh with you
and confront only your empty chair.

Flowers, Two Cats and a Butterfly, mixed media on paper, 14" x 16 ½"

Two Owls in a Tree, mixed media on paper, 16 ½" x 20 ½"

Two Owls in a Tree

Two owls in a tree look so satisfied, don't they? I swear they're smiling. Where did they come from, these two creatures I painted in bright orange on a branch. I, who like Emerson, prefer to watch nature through a window. I, who have never seen an owl, except on "Nature" on PBS, I, who probably would die of fear if these owls, that sprang from my imagination, were to leap off those branches and fly toward me.

Jersey Diners

All the Jersey diners have vanished, those old silver
rectangles with their counter stools that twirled, their
neon lights, their metal tables and fake leather booths.
After we'd go out with a crowd we'd always end up
at one of those diners, each group wanting to stop
at a different one—West's Diner on Rte. 46 in Little Falls,
Libby's in Paterson, Madison Avenue diner near
Railroad Avenue. Looking back, I see our young faces
lit by the harsh diner lights,

and only from a distance do we know how protected
we were, how we'd mourn the passage of time,
the loss of so many we loved,
the vanishing of these diners, replaced by malls
and shopping centers, hotels and big box stores,
the diners glowing only in memory, in all their tacky
glory and we, our faces still untouched by grief and loss,
caught and framed in the diner's windows.

Pensive Woman and Roses, mixed media on paper, 20 ½" x 16 ½"

WE USED TO PLAY SCRABBLE

We used to play Scrabble, and gin rummy and Monopoly.
Once when I was pregnant with our son, you and I played
Monopoly and when I lost, I started to cry.
"Oh, it's okay, it's okay, you can win. Here, here," you said,
handing me bunches of money. Even now, when our son is
a grown man with children of his own who are grown, I am
horrified at how inconsolable I was over losing a game.

Later on, when our children were in grammar school, we'd play
board games with our friends. We were still young and you
weren't sick yet. I remember those evenings, sweet and perfect,
encased in a glass bubble that shimmers and shines. When you
pass my chair you touch the back of my neck or shoulder. One
of our friends is witty and he makes us laugh. Last night, you
tell me that Loretta, the Jamaican woman who takes care
of you, is angry and wants to quit, because the hours
are too long and you don't want to go to bed early enough.
"I didn't want to tell you," you say,
and I know you are afraid.

I tell you I will take care of it when I get home, try to erase
the sadness and humiliation from your voice and wish I could
transport us back to the days when we were young
and laughing over scrabble or gin rummy, our children
giggling on the stairs.

WINTER AT WEST LONG BRANCH, NEW JERSEY

I look out of the window at the deep
blue gray of the ocean, the pampas grass,
the gray roof of the deck, the sky
with its painted clouds. How soothing

it is to watch the water move in its slow
way, to feel the world wind down
from its frantic pace, to lift my face to light
so clear it scrubs the world clean.

THE CHILDREN PLAY

Last night my friend's daughter walks into the living room
holding a toy cat, her arm coiled around her as though
the cat was a baby, the creature cuddled into her chest,
her head bent forward so her lips are nearly touching
the cat's head. When I look closer the cat's paws rest
on the child's chest, the paws moving up and down
just as a real cat's might, marking the child as her own.
Later, at the party, the children run through the kitchen
into the living room following one another,
each additional party guest's child adding to the line
they make as they circle the grown-up chatter.
Gradually they tire of the circle they've made,
and the children break off into groups of two, and I
see my friend's daughter playing seriously
with another child as they work a toy castle
that requires one of them to put an object in a slot
and the other one to catch it as it comes out
the other side. Watching them, I am reminded of my
own daughter at five, the delicate, precise way she
moved her hands, as this child does, and I think
of my daughter today and how much of what she was
when she was five is still part of her, that need to do
things exactly the right way, that desire to be perfect.
I wonder if this child, too, will carry her five-year-old
self with her all her life, as my daughter does,
never losing that way of touching the world
around her with such careful hands.

I Am on the Road Back to Childhood

I am on the road back to childhood, back
to 17th Street and the tenement with the fake
brick siding, back to Zio Guillermo's garden
with corn and tomatoes and zucchini and peppers
and zinnias and marigolds and basil and rosemary,
that fragrant place that made us sure that we lived
in the country. I am on the road back to the 17th Street
kitchen with its big black coal stove and the dangling
one-bulb fixture that lit the table, back to the games
of Monopoly and dominoes and gin rummy that I
played with my sister and brother, back to the aroma
of my mother's homemade bread, back to the meals
she prepared—polenta and spaghetti and meatballs
and sausage and farina—back to the noisy, cheerful
kitchen full of political arguments and laughter, full
of the talk of aunts and uncles, espresso and anisette,
back to small water glasses of wine, back to my father
mixing eggnog for me in a cup, back to my mother sitting
in her rocker, we children leaning over her while she told
us fairy tales from Italy, though her hands were busy
sewing the lining in coats that were dropped off
by the factory each morning and picked up again
the next day, back to a time when we were unaware
of all we didn't have because the arms of our family
were around us and we did not have a TV, that window
into the rest of America, so we were happy with playing tag
in the vacant lot or hide-and-seek in the street, happy
with the evenings on our back stoop where we spoke
in whispers and the neighborhood kids gathered
and summer was an ocean of time we were sure
would never run dry, and the stars, the stars
in the Paterson sky, shone above us, clear and bright
as the future we were sure we could reach out
and hold in our hands.

Women in Bright Dresses, mixed media on paper, 20 ½" x 16 ½"

My Dreams Are Full of Women

My dreams are full of women in bright dresses; they swirl around a room filled with bright lights and birds. Children are there, too. The women look at me as though they want to tell me something. "We are alive," they seem to say. We are together on this canvas and our happiness is so real, we can hold it in our hands. "Here," they say, as they reach toward me, "here take it. We want to give it to you. It's so sweet, isn't it? So sweet, and we are grateful."

OTHER BOOKS BY MARIA MAZZIOTTI GILLAN

Flowers from the Tree of Night, Chantry Press, 1980

Winter Light, Chantry Press, 1985

Luce D'Inverno, Cross-Cultural Communications, 1987

The Weather of Old Seasons, Cross-Cultural Communications, 1987

Taking Back My Name, Malafemmina Press, 1990; Lincoln Springs Press, 1991, repeated printings

Where I Come From: Selected and New Poems, Guernica Editions, 1995, 1997

Things My Mother Told Me, Guernica Editions, 1999

Italian Women in Black Dresses, Guernica Editions, 2002, 2003, 2004

Maria Mazziotti Gillan: Greatest Hits 1972-2002, Pudding House Publications, 2003

Talismans/Talismani, Ibiskos Editions, 2006

All That Lies Between Us, Guernica Editions, 2007

Nightwatch, Poems by Maria Mazziotti and Aeronwy Thomas, The Seventh Quarry Press, 2010

Moments in the Past That Shine, The Ridgeway Press, 2010

What We Pass On: Collected Poems: 1980-2009, Guernica Editions, 2010

The Place I Call Home, NYQ Books, 2012

Writing Poetry to Save Your Life: How to Find the Courage to Tell Your Stories, MiroLand, Guernica, 2013

The Silence in an Empty House, NYQ Books, 2013

Ancestors' Song, Bordighera Press, 2013

Made in the USA
Middletown, DE
25 February 2015